CHRISTMAS

Clare Chandler

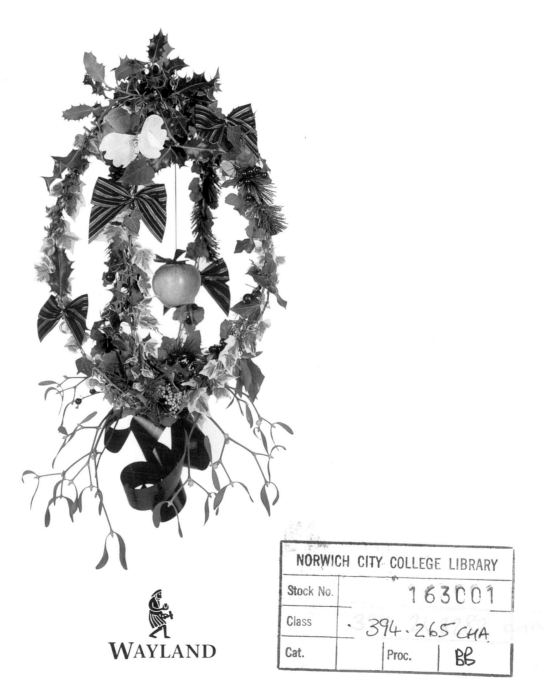

WAYLAND

CARNIVAL

CHINESE NEW YEAR

DIWALI

ID-UL-FITR

PASSOVER

Editors: Polly Goodman/Sarah Doughty
Designer: Tim Mayer

First published in 1996 by Wayland Publishers Ltd
61 Western Road, Hove, East Sussex BN3 1JD

British Library Cataloguing in Publication Data
Chandler, Clare
    Christmas. – (Festival)
    1. Christmas – Juvenile Literature
    I. Title
    394.2'68282

ISBN 0 7502 1846 0

Printed and bound by L.E.G.O. S.p.A.,
Vicenza, Italy

Picture acknowledgements
Associated Press/Topham/J Bouju 26 (top);
Cephas/J.Riviere 20; Mary Evans Picture Library
8, 9, 10, 11, 12 (both); Eye Ubiquitous/Laurence
Fordyce) 29; Sally and Richard Greenhill 19;
Christine Osborne 4, 18 (top), 23, 26 (bottom),
28, cover bottom right; Topham Picturepoint
13, 14, 15, 17 (top), 18 (bottom), 22, 24, cover
bottom left, top left and right; Trip/C. Caffrey
5, 6, A. Tjagny 4,7, V. Kolpakov 17, Trip 17
(bottom), A. Tjagny 21, I. Souriment 5, 25,
A.Tjagny-Rjadno 27; Wayland Picture Library/Paul
Seheult 25 (top) and title page, Tim Woodcock 29
(bottom). Border artwork by Tim Mayer.

CONTENTS

◄ A Christmas service in a Russian Orthodox church in Moscow. For many years, during Communist rule, Christians in Russia and Eastern Europe were not allowed to hold church services. But now they are enjoying the freedom to worship as they please.

▲ In Germany, groups of boys like this, some dressed as the wise men, parade through the streets of the towns at Christmas carrying a star, singing carols known as star-songs.

▲ A Christmas service at Bethlehem in Jordan, the town where Jesus was born. These are Orthodox Christians so, unlike Western Christians, they celebrate Christmas on 6 January.

▲ In Goa, western India, Christians have a big celebration at Epiphany on 6 January. Children dressed as the wise men ride up to the church on donkeys, where everyone from the village joins in with a great feast.

▲ The inside of this Catholic church in New York is decorated with Christmas trees and Poinsettia plants. Statues of Jesus, the Virgin Mary and the saints are often found in Catholic churches.

▲ A family in Korea is celebrating Christmas. Like countless other Christians all over the world, they have dressed in their finest clothes for this special day and have exchanged presents next to the Christmas tree.

Nativity scenes like this, including figures of Mary, Joseph and the three wise men, can be found in town squares across North and Central America. This one is in the town of Guadalajara in Mexico. ▼

◄ Christmas is celebrated in December or early January all over the world. So in countries like Australia in the southern hemisphere, Christmas Day falls at the height of summer. Families there often enjoy their Christmas dinner out of doors, either as a barbecue in the garden or a picnic on the beach.

THE STORY OF JESUS' BIRTH

The Roman Emperor Augustus had ordered a census to be taken throughout the Roman Empire. Everyone had to go and register in their own town.

Joseph went with Mary from Nazareth in Galilee to Bethlehem. Mary was pregnant, and while they were in Bethlehem, she gave birth to her baby, Jesus. There was no room for them to stay at an inn so Jesus was born in a stable. Mary wrapped him in strips of cloth and laid him in a manger.

The word 'Christmas' makes people imagine all sorts of good things – twinkling lights, buying presents, the rustle of wrapping paper, Christmas foods and decorations, the special atmosphere of a candlelit church or the excitement of Christmas Eve. These are some of the traditions that make Christmas, for many people, the best-loved time of the year.

In many parts of the world Christmas is a national holiday and it is a special time for people, whether they are Christians or not. However, for Christians, Christmas is a very important festival. They believe that God came to earth as a baby, Jesus, and was born in a stable 2,000 years ago. That is what is remembered at Christmas. Many Christians go to church to celebrate the birthday of Jesus Christ.

Nativity scenes like this, in Mexico, illustrate the story of Jesus' birth in a stable.

The word Christmas comes from 'Christ's Mass' – a church service held every year, usually on 25 December. The period of Advent leads up to Christmas, a time when the Church prepares for the coming of Jesus Christ. The Christmas festival lasts from Christmas Eve until 6 January. These 12 days are a time of feasting and fun when people try to be cheerful and friendly towards each other. They send cards and give presents, eat special foods and have parties with their friends and families.

There are many traditions connected with Christmas, and each country has its own special festivities. In some parts of the world Christmas takes place in the middle of winter, while other places are enjoying the height of summer. This means there are many different ways of celebrating at Christmas, but everyone believes that, above all, it is a time for peace and goodwill to other people.

An Orthodox Christmas service in a church in Moscow. Paintings on the wall of the church usually show Jesus, Mary or the saints. They are important to Orthodox Christians who believe that they help them to worship.

THE HISTORY OF CHRISTMAS

People have been holding festivals at the end of the year for over 4,000 years. The end of December in the northern hemisphere is the depth of winter, when days are short and the sun is at its weakest. Ancient peoples, who depended on the sun to grow their food, held mid-winter festivals at this time. They did not understand the seasons and were never sure that the sun would grow strong again, so they lit fires and held ceremonies to encourage the sun to return.

In northern Europe these festivities were called Yule.

Saturnalia was an important festival for the Romans. Many of the ways in which they celebrated have become part of Christmas festivities today.

The Romans called their winter festival Saturnalia after their god of the harvest, Saturn. Saturnalia was held between 17 and 28 December and was a holiday for everyone. Schools were closed and slaves were free to do and say as they liked. Everyone enjoyed feasting and wild merry-making. During Saturnalia, a mock king was appointed who represented the god, Saturn, and led the festivities.

In the fourth century, Christianity became the official religion of the Roman Empire. The old customs that were developed in mid-winter festivals gradually became a part of celebrating Christ's birthday.

THE LORD OF MISRULE

In the courts of the Middle Ages there was a similar Christmas custom to the mock king of Saturnalia – he was called the Lord of Misrule. He was the king for the festive season, planning the games, plays and songs, telling jokes and making fun of everyone.

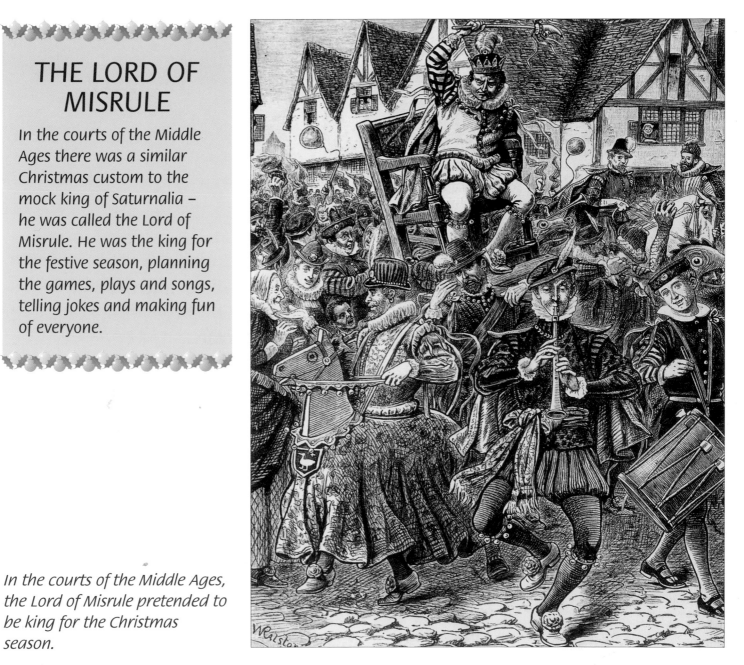

In the courts of the Middle Ages, the Lord of Misrule pretended to be king for the Christmas season.

This picture from an old children's book shows a yule log being dragged home by a group of children. It would then be decorated and kept burning for three days over Christmas.

THE YULE LOG

During the festivities of Yule, many hundreds of years ago, a huge log was dragged home, decorated with greenery and ribbons and kept burning for days. Its magic was thought to restore the power of the sun.

The Yule log tradition has now found a place in Christmas celebrations in some countries in northern Europe. When it dies out the ashes are kept to put on the fields in the belief that they will protect crops from disease.

Some people also eat a chocolate cake in the shape of a Yule log at Christmas.

No one knows the exact date that Jesus Christ was born. The early Christians in Rome decided to celebrate Christ's birthday at the time of the festival of Saturnalia. The Pope said that Christmas Day should be celebrated on 25 December and gradually this custom became widespread.

In Europe, in the sixteenth century, many people who belonged to the Catholic Church became Protestant. The new Church disapproved of many of the old customs, and processions, statues and colourful ceremonies were forbidden. Christmas became very serious and dull. In England, in the sixteenth century, Christmas was abolished altogether but was brought back later with much merry-making.

The first settlers in America, who came from England in the sixteenth century, were Protestants called Puritans. They believed that everything about their lives should be very plain and they would not allow any festivities at Christmas.

It was only with the arrival of immigrants from Europe in the nineteenth century, who brought their traditions with them, that such festivities became accepted throughout America as part of the celebration of Christmas.

A Puritan governor puts a stop to Christmas celebrations in North America in the nineteenth century. Neither playing games nor drinking were allowed during the Christmas period.

CHRISTMAS STORIES

Over the years, magical stories have been made up about Christmas which have been passed on from generation to generation. The best Christmas stories are about someone who secretly brings presents to children. This person has different names in different countries but the best known is Santa Claus or Father Christmas. On Christmas Eve, Santa Claus is said to ride through the night sky on his sleigh pulled by reindeer. Gliding down on to the rooftops, he goes down the chimneys leaving presents for every child.

This is a Victorian image of Father Christmas, with his long red robes and sleigh pulled by reindeer. Present-day pictures of him are very similar.

In Sweden, the festival of St. Lucia on 13 December marks the beginning of the Christmas season. The youngest girl in the house wears a white dress and a crown of candles on her head. She takes coffee and cakes to the rest of her family.

The legend of Santa Claus began in the Netherlands. The name comes from the Dutch for 'St. Nicholas' which is Sinterklaas. St. Nicholas was a bishop and a rich man living in the third century who used his wealth to help other people. Father Christmas is similar to Santa Claus – they both have long white beards and dress in red robes – but Father Christmas is an old British legend.

Another favourite Christmas story is about a Swedish saint. Little is known about St. Lucia, but she is supposed to have been put to death for being a Christian in the fourth century. After her death it is thought that she become a star in the sky. A feast day for St. Lucia is held in Sweden on 13 December.

A nineteenth-century card showing St. Nicholas. St. Nicholas was Bishop of Myra in Asia Minor. He was very generous to poor people and the legend of Santa Claus, secret bringer of presents to children, is based on his story.

THE THORN TREE OF GLASTONBURY

A thirteenth-century story about Saint Joseph of Arimathea tells how he went to Glastonbury and planted his walking stick on a hill there. It grew into a thorn tree which flowered every Christmas and people came from far away to see the amazing sight of the buds bursting into flower in the middle of winter.

In the north of Italy there is a Christmas story of an ugly witch called Befana. Befana lived in Bethlehem where Jesus was born. Although she knew about his birth, Befana delayed going to see Jesus until it was too late and he had left. Since then, Befana has been wandering all over the world looking for the baby Jesus, leaving a present at every house just in case he is there.

The Russians have a similar story about a woman called Baboushka. It is said that Baboushka entertained the wise men on their way to Bethlehem. When they told her that they were on their way to see the greatest king on earth she wanted to go with them.

An artist's impression of the ugly witch, Befana. A story tells how she is supposed to bring presents to children in Italy at Epiphany, on 6 January.

Baboushka urged the wise men to wait until morning so that she could do the housework first, but they said they must travel at night because they were guided by a wonderful bright star.

THE MIRACLE OF THE POINSETTIA

The story of the Poinsettia plant comes from Mexico. It was the custom there for people to take a gift for Jesus to the church on Christmas Eve. The story says that there was one little girl who was very poor and had nothing to take. As she stood outside the church wondering what to do, an angel appeared and told her to pick some weeds by the church door and take them in. Everyone laughed at her as she walked into the church carrying a bunch of weeds. But then, to everyone's amazement, the top leaves of each stem turned bright red.

Since then the weeds, which are called Poinsettias, have been a traditional Christmas plant in many countries.

That evening, after they set off, Baboushka cleaned her house. The next morning she tried to follow the wise men but, because it was daylight, the star could no longer be seen and she lost her way.

By the time she reached Bethlehem, Mary, Joseph and the baby, Jesus, had already left. The story says that, even to this day, Baboushka, too, is wandering the world looking for the baby, calling at each house and leaving a gift for every child.

Like Befana in Italy, Baboushka is said to leave gifts for each child in Russia just in case they are the baby Jesus.

CUSTOMS

Stories and legends about Christmas have survived and spread around the world. In some countries Father Christmas, or Santa Claus is known by every child. Children meet 'Father Christmas' in stores and grottos, and post him letters asking for presents. All around the world shopping arcades are decked with presents and cards in time for Christmas. Part of the fun of Christmas is the excitement that builds up before Christmas Day.

Children in Britain and the USA hang stockings on the ends of their beds or by the fireplace on Christmas Eve (24 December) for Santa Claus, or Father Christmas, to fill with presents. Dutch children leave their shoes by the fireplace on 5 December for Sinterklaas to come down the chimney and fill them with little gifts. Many European countries give their presents on the Eve of St Nicholas' Day, which is 6 December. German children find gifts under the tree on Christmas Eve from Christkindl, the Christ child. In Italy, children receive presents from the witch Befana on 6 January.

All over the world, children visit Father Christmas in grottos, shops and at Christmas parties like this one in Latvia.

One of the most exciting things about Christmas is waking up to find a stocking (or shoe) filled with presents from Santa Claus.

Christmas customs vary from family to family, town to town and country to country. In many parts of the world present-giving is an essential part of Christmas. People give presents to their family and friends to show that they like them and to make them happy. In many African countries, however, people think less about giving and receiving presents at Christmas and more about visiting and entertaining friends. In Ghana, young men make Christmas huts out of coconut palms away from the family home in which to entertain their friends. At Christmas, fireworks light up the sky all over Africa.

A family in Korea open their presents on Christmas Day.

PIÑATAS

Mexican children play a special Christmas game called Piñatas. Small clay jars, decorated to look like animals or birds, are filled with little presents and sweets and hung from the trees. Wearing blindfolds, children try to hit the piñatas with a stick. If they break, all the children scramble to collect the gifts that shower down.

Other customs take place every year. Many of these customs, such as nativity plays, have a religious meaning and people have been observing them for hundreds of years. Nativity plays began in the thirteenth century as part of the Miracle Plays, which told stories from the Bible. Plays about the nativity are put on by children in infant schools, where they act out the story of Jesus' birth.

Christians celebrate Jesus's birth in a church in Bethlehem. This is an Orthodox service in which the congregation stands.

At Christmas special songs are sung, called carols. A carol has come to mean a song about the nativity story. They are sung not only in churches, but by people gathering in all sorts of places.

In many countries, it is the custom for groups of singers to go from house to house, where they are rewarded with gifts of money, food or drinks.

In Germany, groups of boys, one leading carrying a gold star on a pole, and the others dressed as the wise men, walk through the streets singing carols known as star-songs.

Carol singers like this, called star-singers, are a common sight in German towns. One of the boys, dressed as a king, carries a present for the baby Jesus.

Christians celebrate Christmas Eve by going to a midnight mass or service, and on Christmas Day religious festivals are held to celebrate Christ's birth. In Orthodox churches, mostly in eastern Europe, the mass is held on 6 January. The Orthodox Church celebrates Christian festivals at different times and in different ways from other Christian Churches, usually 13 days later.

Children dress up as Joseph, Mary, the wise men, shepherds, angels and sometimes even the stable animals, for the school nativity play. They act out the story of Jesus' birth for the rest of the school and their families to watch.

The day after Christmas Day, 26 December, is known as Boxing Day, though no one is sure why. It may be because boxes were put in churches during the Christmas season to collect and distribute money for poor people; or they may have been servant's 'tips' opened on 26 December.

GOOD KING WENCESLAS

This carol is about a king who lived over 1,000 years ago in a country called Bohemia, which is now part of the Czech Republic. King Wenceslas was the first Christian ruler of his country and the carol tells of his kindness to a poor man on the feast of Saint Stephen on 26 December, when he gave the poor man food and shelter. It is said that although it was a freezing cold night, the air around the king was so warm that the snow melted where he trod.

FEASTING

Christmas has always been a time for feasting. In many countries the main celebration is a delicious dinner on Christmas Day. People usually eat a roast turkey, goose or duck, followed by a pudding made from dried fruits. In the past, when people made their own puddings rather than buying them from a shop all the family took it in turns to stir the pudding-mixture and make a wish. Little charms were often added to the mixture, such as old sixpenny pieces, which were believed to bring good luck to whoever found one in their portion. Whether it is bought or made, the Christmas pudding is still soaked in brandy, set alight and put on the table with blue flames dancing around it.

SACRED BREAD

In Latvia, bread has always been a very important food and, as a symbol of Christ's body, it is considered sacred. Latvian children are taught from a very early age that, if a piece of bread falls on the floor, it has to be picked up and kissed in apology.

The Latvian Christmas speciality are delicious bacon-filled turnovers, or rolls, called piragi.

In many countries a roast turkey is the usual Christmas dinner. In Britain it is often eaten like this, with little sausages and bacon rolls, lots of vegetables and cranberry sauce.

In some countries, people eat their special meal on Christmas Eve. In Poland, people wait for the first star to appear in the sky on Christmas Eve, then they eat a meal of fish. A wafer of bread, called an oplatek, which has a picture of the nativity scene impressed on it, is passed around and everyone breaks off a piece. Hay is spread all around the room to remind everyone that Jesus was born in a stable and extra places are set at the table for Mary and the Christ-child.

Champagne flows as a Russian family in Moscow share a special Christmas meal. This would normally include pork and sauerkraut.

Each country has its own traditional Christmas food. In Norway, children bake thaw biscuits (the heat from all the ovens baking is supposed to thaw the snow). And in countries in the southern hemisphere, like Australia, where it is summer in December, Christmas dinner is often a barbecue or a picnic of cold turkey on the beach.

These pastries, made with almonds and hazel nuts, dried fruits, including figs, and chocolate, are a Christmas delicacy in the south of Italy.

Children in the Netherlands make a special cake called Letterbanket to eat on Christmas Eve. This is a mixture of pastry and marzipan, made into the shapes of the initials of each person in the family.

Mince pies are an old favourite in many countries at Christmas. Hundreds of years ago they used to be made with meat that was flavoured with spices – ginger, cinnamon, cloves and nutmeg – to disguise the fact that the meat was not very fresh. The pastry used to be made in the shape of a manger, sometimes with a little figure of a baby on top. Gradually the meat disappeared and nowadays the 'mincemeat' is made from dried fruits. In Italy, people eat something similar called bucellato, which is a hollow doughnut-shape of pastry filled with mincemeat, minced figs, nuts and chocolate.

In Denmark people eat a special meal on Christmas Eve. After the main course of pork or duck and little potatoes coated with melted butter and sugar, they eat an unusual pudding. It is a sort of rice pudding made with cream and hidden inside it is a single almond nut. Whoever is lucky enough to get the almond in their portion of pudding gets a present as well.

All over Scandinavia an alcoholic drink called schnapps is popular. It is very strong and is served freezing cold with a glass of beer. In other countries people like to have a hot drink called mulled wine at Christmas. The wine is warmed up and flavoured with sugar and spices.

A CHRISTMAS FEAST IN THE MIDDLE AGES

A rich person's Christmas feast in the Middle Ages, in Europe, would often last all day. As well as a whole boar's head, they would eat swan, little birds, partridges, venison and goose. The highlight of the meal was a roast peacock. The peacock's skin, including its feathers, was taken off carefully before it was cooked. Then the skin was put back on, the beak painted gold and a taper put in its mouth and set alight.

The table was laden with vast pies, bowls of wassail and huge ships and castles made out of sugar.

This is a big family get-together for a Christmas meal in a garden in Australia.

THE HOLLY AND THE IVY

Decorating the house with evergreens is a very ancient tradition. Long ago, people believed that these plants had magical powers because they stayed green all through the year when most plants lost their leaves. The Romans draped their halls in ivy and laurel leaves during Saturnalia, and it is still the custom in many places for people to fill their houses with evergreens at Christmas. Holly, especially, is used at Christmas because it is a symbol of the crown of thorns that was put on Christ's head when he died. The sharp prickles are like the thorns and the red berries are like drops of blood.

Although mistletoe is found in many peoples' homes at Christmas, it is not used to decorate churches. This is because in pre-Christian times, it was used by Druids in northern Europe as a holy plant to worship the gods. Mistletoe grows in trees, including the oak, which was the Druids' sacred tree. Druids believed that the evergreen mistletoe kept the spirit of the tree alive during the winter. They would cut it with a golden sickle as a thanksgiving for the spring to come. Ever since, it has been hung in doorways to show goodwill to visitors, and a person can claim a kiss from anyone they choose under the mistletoe.

When Jesus was crucified, a crown of thorns was put on his head, as shown in this painting. The holly that people decorate their houses with at Christmas is meant to symbolize the crown of thorns. The berries represent drops of blood.

MAKE A KISSING BOUGH

You will need:
  2 or 3 wire coathangers
    evergreen foliage including holly and mistletoe
  red ribbon
    string and green sticky tape

1. Bend the coathangers into hoops and tie them
   together with string at the top. Tape the hooks
   together and stick tape over the joins.
2. Bind the evergreens onto the wires using sticky tape
to hold them in place. Hang a piece of mistletoe at
the bottom.
3. Tie bows with the ribbon at the top and the bottom.
4. Hang your kissing bough where people can stand
   underneath it.

The plants in the foreground of
this picture of a church in New
York are Poinsettias. They are
popular Christmas plants in
many parts of the world.

For hundreds of years it has been the custom in Germany to bring in another evergreen – the fir tree – and decorate it. The idea spread to Britain in Victorian times. Today, an enormous tree stands in Trafalgar Square in the heart of London at Christmas, covered with lights, and crowds gather around it to sing carols. Another huge tree grows outside the White House in Washington D.C., in the USA. Every year, at Christmas, the President of the USA switches on the lights that decorate it.

Despite the rain, crowds gather by the Christmas tree in Trafalgar Square, London, to sing carols under their umbrellas.

The beginning of the Christmas season in many countries is signalled by the 'lighting up' of town centres where elaborate displays of lights brighten the shopping areas. Strings of lights are used to decorate houses and trees outside, while inside, rooms are often lit by the softer glow of candlelight. Candles have long been used at Christmas, either as a symbol of the coming of spring, or to represent the birth of Christ – the 'Light of the World'. Light and hope are symbolized by candles on the Advent wreath and on the Christingle.

Life-sized models of the holy family make up a nativity scene outside a church in Arizona, USA.

Candles are used in many countries at Christmas because they symbolize hope and the birth of Jesus – the 'Light of the World'. These candles are in a church in Moscow, Russia.

The Christingle is a decorated orange, often made by children at Christmas. The orange represents Jesus as the light of the world, with fruit, nuts and sweets put around the top to show the four corners of the world and the good things within it.

Model cribs have also been a part of Christmas decorations for hundreds of years. The nativity scene is recreated with figures of Mary, Joseph, the baby Jesus lying in a manger, the animals, shepherds and wise men. The idea of a crib was started by St. Francis of Assisi in Italy, in the twelfth century. Today cribs are popular all over the world. In America, open-air Nativity scenes, called Christmas Gardens, decorate public spaces of some cities.

Christmas decorations are taken down on Twelfth Night, the last day of Christmas – 6 January. To leave them up is supposed to bring bad luck to the household for the coming year. The date of 6 January is also Epiphany. Epiphany marks the end of Christmas, but it is also a Christian festival in itself which remembers when Jesus was shown to the wise men.

THE CHRISTIAN CALENDAR

Advent *December*

The Christian Church begins its year in December with the season of Advent. It lasts just over three weeks and it is the time when people prepare for Christmas. Many children have Advent calendars which have 24 or 25 windows to open. They open a window each day to see the picture inside.

Christmas *December*

Christmas is the festival when Jesus Christ's birth is celebrated. It lasts for 12 days. Christmas Day is on 25 December, although Orthodox Christians celebrate Christmas on 6 January.

Epiphany *6 January* ▶

Epiphany is the last of the 12 days of Christmas. Epiphany means 'showing', and it celebrates the story of Jesus being shown to the wise men who had travelled to see the new baby king.

Shrove Tuesday

This is the day before the beginning of Lent. It is also known as Pancake Day. People used to make pancakes to use up foods like fat and eggs which would go off during Lent when everyone was fasting. Shrove Tuesday is known in many countries by its French name, Mardi Gras, which means 'Fat Tuesday'. It is celebrated with a carnival which sometimes lasts for a week beforehand.

Lent *Spring*

Lent takes place during the 6 weeks before Easter. It is the time when Christians feel sorry for anything they have done wrong and try to make a new start in their lives. It used to be a time for fasting, and many people still give up something they enjoy during Lent.

Good Friday

Good Friday is a very solemn day when Christians remember that Jesus died on the cross. ▼

Easter Sunday

Easter is when Christians celebrate that Jesus came back to life again. In many countries eggs are eaten because they are a symbol of new life. In the Orthodox Church, services are held at midnight as Easter Day begins. The dark church is gradually filled with lighted candles as a symbol that the 'Light of the World' has returned.

Ascension Day

Ascension Day is 40 days after Easter. It is the day when Jesus was last seen on earth.

Pentecost

The Day of Pentecost was the time when Jesus' disciples were given the power of the Holy Spirit to guide them in their work of telling everyone about God. Many Christians hold processions on this day. It is also known as Whit Sunday.

Harvest festival

September or October

Churches are decorated with fruit, vegetables and sheaves of corn as well as flowers at harvest festival because it is a time when people thank God for the harvest and for providing them with food. ▼

GLOSSARY

Bohemia
An old country that is now part of the Czech Republic.

Catholic Church
The Christian Church ruled by the Pope in Rome, Italy.

Census
A way of finding out how many people there are in a country, and any specific information about them.

Druids
Priests in ancient Europe.

Epiphany
The last of the 12 days of Christmas.

Evergreen
A word used to describe plants which keep their leaves through the winter.

Grottos
Small caves, especially ones with attractive features that have been made for a purpose.

Hemisphere
Half of the Earth. The northern and southern hemispheres are divided by an imaginary line called the equator.

Immigrant
A settler in a foreign country.

Nativity story
The story of the birth of Christ.

Orthodox Christians
People who belong to the Russian or Greek Orthodox Church. They are Christians but they have different forms of worship from the Western Church and have a different calendar.

Protestant Church
The Church which broke away from the Catholic Church in the 1500s and is no longer ruled by the Pope.

Roman Empire
All the countries that the Romans conquered and controlled during the 500 years after Christ was born.

Sauerkraut
A dish of pickled cabbage.

Taper
A spill; a thin strip of wax or card for transferring a flame.

Wassail
An alcoholic drink at Christmas, especially spiced beer or mulled wine. Wassailing can also mean to go carol singing at Christmas.

BOOKS TO READ

Christmas by R. Thomson
(Watts,1994)

Christmas by T. Wood
(A & C Black, 1991)

Christmas Poetry, selected by
Robert Hull (Wayland, 1991)

Poems for Christmas, compiled by
J. Bennett (Scholastic, 1992)

Winter Festivals by M. Rosen
(Wayland, 1990)

USEFUL ADDRESSES

To find out more about Christianity,
you may find these addresses useful:

The British Council of Churches,
2 Eaton Gate, London, SW1W 9BT.

Catholic Information Service,
74 Gallow Hill Lane, Abbotts
Langley, Herts, WD5 OBZ.

Christian Education Movement,
2 Chester House, Pages Lane,
London, N10 1PR.

Church of England Information
Office, Church House, Deans Yard,
London, SW1P 3NZ.

Committee for Extra-Diocesan
Affairs, Russian Orthodox Cathedral,
Ennismore Gardens, London SW7.

Society of Friends, Friends House,
Euston Road, London, NW1 2BJ.

INDEX